What's That Noise?

Sally Prue
Illustrated by Desideria Guicciardini

Ryan liked playing with his trains.

"Look at all these trains!" said Dad.

"I'll put them away," said Ryan.

"Then it's bedtime," said Mum.

That night, Ryan had a dream. He dreamed that some men were digging a hole. It was so big that a giant rabbit hopped out of it. The rabbit had big feet that banged on the ground.

Bang! Bang! BANG!

Ryan woke up. The giant white rabbit had gone. But something was still going bang! Bang! BANG!

"Mum!" shouted Ryan. The banging stopped.

"Mum, what was all that banging?" asked Ryan.

"It's nothing," said Mum. "Go back to sleep."

The next day, everything was quiet. Ryan came home from school and played with his trains. Then he had dinner.

“What was all that banging last night?” he asked Dad.

“I don’t know,” said Dad. “Maybe it was the water pipes.

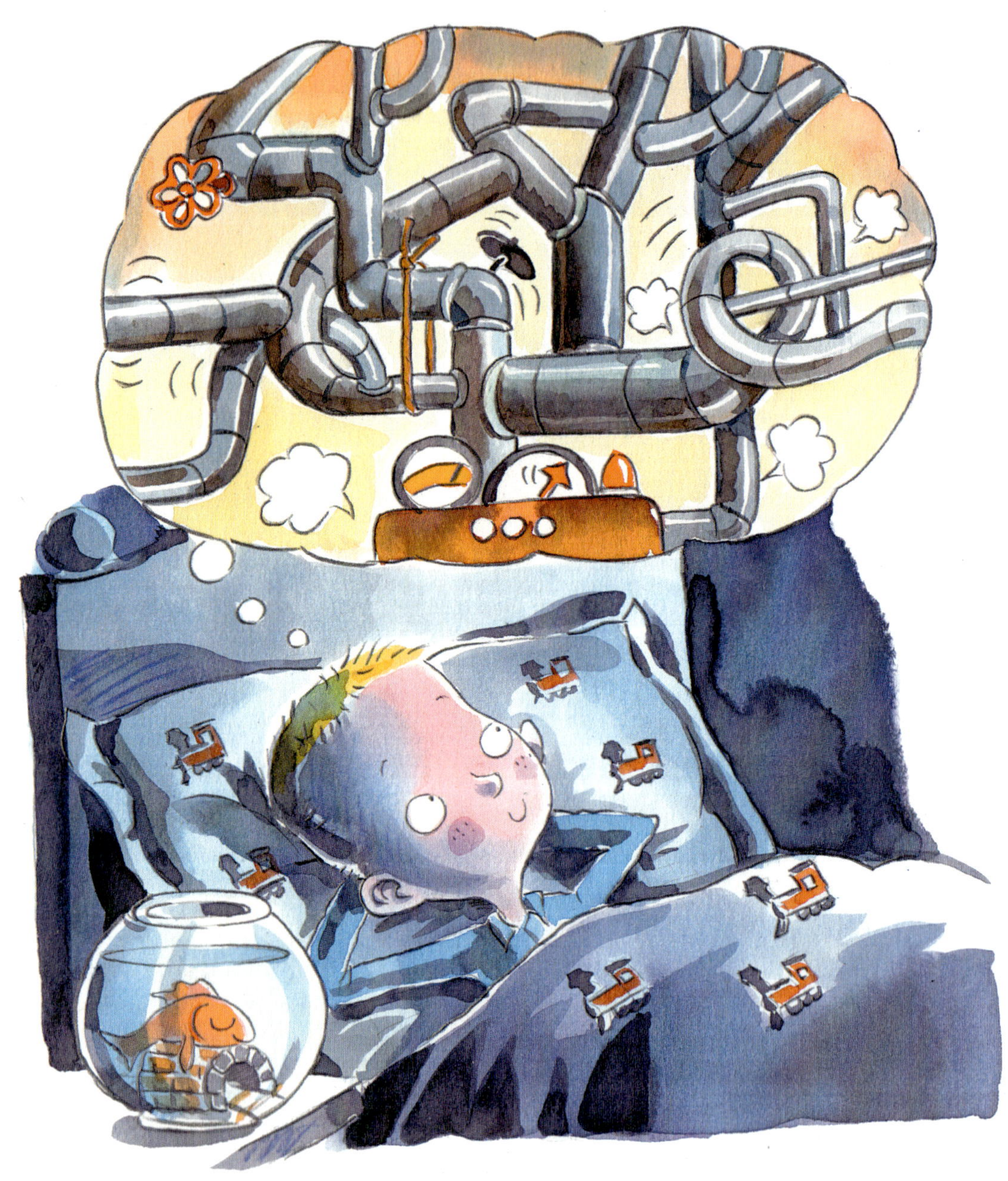

That night, Ryan heard the banging again. He was glad it was just the water pipes.

Bang! Bang! Bang! went the water pipes. Bang! Bang! OUCH!

"What was that?" thought Ryan.

The next day, everything was quiet. Ryan came home from school and played with his trains. Then he had dinner.

“That banging came back last night,” said Ryan. “It went ‘ouch’!”

“Well, it could have been the cat,” said Dad, “with a bad foot.”

That night, the banging was worse! BANG! BANG! BANG!

Ryan couldn't sleep. Something terrible must be going on.

The next day, everything was quiet. Ryan came home from school, but he was too tired to play with his trains.

"I want to sleep down here tonight," said Ryan. "Away from the banging."

"It's all right," said Dad. "The banging will stop. I have something to show you. Come with me!"

Ryan and Dad went up the ladder.

"A train layout!" said Ryan. "You've made me a train layout!"

Ryan was so happy he jumped up and down. Bang! Bang! BANG! went his feet on the floor. And he didn't mind a bit.